Contents

T0351686

Written by
Alison Hawes
Illustrated by
Stephen Elford

Series editor **Dee Reid**

P **Pearson**

Characters

Tom

Anna

Mrs Barnes

A policeman

Two ambulance men

Tricky words

- freezing
- through
- listened
- reply
- ambulance
- moaned
- duvet
- siren

Read these words to the student. Help them with these words when they appear in the text

Introduction

It was freezing cold and getting dark in Aspen Road and Tom was helping Anna to do her paper round when they heard someone calling for help. The sound was coming from the garden. They climbed over the gate and found Mrs Barnes lying on the path. Her eyes were closed and she was very still.

You've Got It Wrong!

It was getting dark and Tom was freezing cold.
"Come on!" he said, as Anna pushed the paper
through Mrs Barnes' letter box.
"No, wait! I think I can hear something," said Anna.

Tom went up to the door and listened.
"I can't hear a thing," he said. "Come on.
My feet are freezing!"
"No! Sssh! Listen!" said Anna.

Someone was calling for help.
"It's coming from the garden," said Tom.
He banged on the locked gate.
"Mrs Barnes, are you ok?" he called.
But there was no reply.

Tom and Anna climbed over the gate.
Mrs Barnes was lying on the path.
Her eyes were closed and she was very still.

"She must have slipped on the ice," said Tom.
Anna pulled her mobile out of her pocket and
called 999.
"Don't worry Mrs Barnes," said Tom. "We're
calling for an ambulance."
Mrs Barnes moaned but did not open her eyes.

Tom bent down next to Mrs Barnes and felt her hand. It was like ice. "She'll freeze to death if we don't do something!" he said.

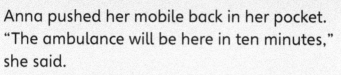

Anna pushed her mobile back in her pocket.
"The ambulance will be here in ten minutes,"
she said.
Then she ran into the house to fetch a duvet.

As they put the duvet round her,
Mrs Barnes opened her eyes.
"My handbag," she said.
"Don't worry about that," said Anna.
"Handbag... Keys... Lock up..."
said Mrs Barnes and closed her eyes.

Tom ran into the house to fetch Mrs Barnes' handbag. He took out her keys and locked the back door.

"Listen!" said Anna. "I can hear a siren." Tom opened the gate and ran out to meet the ambulance.

But the siren was not an ambulance.
A policeman grabbed Tom by the arm.
"Where are you going with that handbag?"
he said, taking it out of Tom's hand.
"No, wait! It's Mrs Barnes' bag. I didn't steal it"
said Tom. "You've got it wrong!"

"I don't think so!" said the policeman, putting Tom in the back of the car. "Someone saw you climb over the gate and they called us," said the policeman, as he locked the car door.

Tom banged on the car window. "Anna! Anna! Help!" he shouted. But Anna couldn't hear him.

An ambulance came down Aspen Road
with its siren on.
It pulled up by the police car and
two ambulance men got out.
"Where is Mrs Barnes?" they asked.
"Who?" said the policeman.

Tom banged on the car window.
"She's in the garden!" he shouted. "She slipped on the ice. My friend called you."

The policeman went very still.
Then he went very red.
He opened the car door and let Tom out.
"I'm sorry, I think I got it wrong!" he said.

Quiz ///////////////

Text comprehension

Literal comprehension
p7 What has happened to Mrs Barnes?
p9 What good idea does Anna have to help Mrs Barnes?

Inferential comprehension
p11 Why does Tom take Mrs Barnes' handbag?
p12 Why did the policeman suspect Tom?
p16 Why did the policeman go very red?

Personal response
- Do you think Tom and Anna should have climbed over Mrs Barnes' gate?
- Do you think Tom will understand why the policeman made the mistake?

Word knowledge

p7 How many syllables in the word 'ambulance'?
p7 Find a word that means 'groaned'.
p8 Find three verbs on this page.

Spelling challenge

Read these words:

getting   wait   about
Now try to spell them!

Ha! Ha! Ha!

What do you give to a person who has everything?

A burglar alarm!

Find out about

- how Adolf Beck and Terry Irving were sent to prison for crimes they didn't commit.

Tricky words

- commit
- innocent
- accused
- jewellery
- panicked
- jury
- guilty
- decided

Read these words to the student. Help them with these words when they appear in the text.

Introduction

Every year some people are sent to prison for crimes they didn't commit. In 1895, a woman accused Adolf Beck of stealing her jewellery and the police believed her. He was put on trial, found guilty and sent to prison for seven years. In Australia in 1993, Terry Irving served five years in prison for a crime he did not commit.

Every year, some people are sent to prison
for crimes they didn't commit.
Some people have to spend years
in prison before they can prove
they were innocent all the time.
This happened to a man called Adolf Beck.

Adolf Beck

In 1895, a woman came up to
Adolf Beck in the street and accused
him of stealing her jewellery.
Adolf told her she must have
confused him with someone else,
but the woman was sure it was
Adolf who had stolen her jewellery.

Adolf panicked and ran away.
But the woman ran after him
shouting that he was a thief.
Then she told the police.
The police believed the woman.

Adolf was put on trial for stealing the woman's jewellery. He kept telling everyone that he was innocent. But no one thought he was telling the truth!
The jury found him guilty and he was sent to prison for seven years.

Three years after Adolf came
out of prison, the same thing
happened to him again!
Another woman accused him
of stealing her jewellery!

Once again, Adolf was put on trial and just like the last time, the jury found him guilty. But luckily, the judge at this trial was not so sure that Adolf was guilty.

The police did some more work and found out that both women had mistaken Adolf for another man who looked just like him.

So, at long last, everyone knew that Adolf Beck really was an innocent man and he was set free.

In Australia, in 1993, a man called Terry Irving was accused of robbing a bank. Terry kept telling everyone that he was innocent. But no one believed him!

Three women who worked in the bank felt sure that Terry was the man who had robbed the bank.
Terry said they had made a mistake but the women felt sure it was him.

The odd thing was that Terry did not look like the photo of the robber from the security camera.
Other people outside the bank did not think Terry was the man they saw going into the bank.
But Terry was **still** found guilty and sent to prison for eight years.

All the time Terry was in prison, he
tried to prove he was innocent.
Then, after he had been in prison for
five years, another court decided Terry
was innocent. So he was set free.

After Adolf was found innocent,
he was given £5,000 for the time
he had spent in prison.
That would be the same as £300,000
in today's money.

But Terry has not been so lucky.
He asked the courts for some
money for the time he spent in
prison, but to this day, he has not
been given a single dollar.

Quiz ////////////////

Text comprehension

Literal comprehension
p20 What did the woman accuse Adolf of doing?
p22 How many years did Adolf spend in prison?

Inferential comprehension
p21 What mistake did Adolf make?
p26 Why did people not believe Terry Irving?
p31 Why might Terry feel more angry than Adolf?

Personal response
p24 How do you think Adolf felt when he was found guilty a second time?
p30 Do you think Adolf thought £5,000 made up for being imprisoned for seven years?

Word knowledge

p19 Find two words which are plurals.
p20 Find a word which means 'muddled'.
p22 How many syllables are there in the word 'innocent'?

Spelling challenge

Read these words:

again   really   near

Now try to spell them!

Ha! Ha! Ha!

Why did the robber take a bath?

Because he wanted to make a clean getaway!